DEMENTIA
Mother's Story

Patsy Barnes

Gotham Books

30 N Gould St.
Ste. 20820, Sheridan, WY 82801
https://gothambooksinc.com/

Phone: 1 (307) 464-7800

© 2023 *Patsy Barnes*. All rights reserved.

No part of this book may be reproduced, stored in a retrieval system, or transmitted by any means without the written permission of the author.

Published by Gotham Books (July 28, 2023)

   ISBN: 979-8-88775-434-5 (P)
   ISBN: 979-8-88775-435-2 (E)

Because of the dynamic nature of the Internet, any web addresses or links contained in this book may have changed since publication and may no longer be valid.

The views expressed in this work are solely those of the author and do not necessarily reflect the views of the publisher, and the publisher hereby disclaims any responsibility for them.

TABLE OF CONTENTS

ONE
GRANDMA IN BAG-KRISTIN 1

TWO
THE BEGINNING 4

THREE
FACTS AND TREATMENT 8

FOUR
HOW DID MOTHERS DOCTORS VISIT GO? 13

FIVE
TRAJECTORY 18

SIX
WOULD YOU EVER 25

SEVEN
WOULD YOU LIKE 28

EIGHT
YOUR MOTHER IS 30

NINE
MOTHER JUST 34

TEN

WHAT HAPPENS.. 40

ELEVEN

HOSPICE.. 43

TWELVE

IN GOOD TIMES... 50

THIRTEEN

DEATH TRAJECTORIES 57

FOURTEEN

THE ENDING... 61

Chapter ONE

GRANDMA IN BAG-KRISTIN

"Grandma's caught in the bag and can't get out!" We had decided that mother was declining more rapidly, so we gathered the grandkids and my sister and I and decided to have a last "work on the house" day. Everyone gathered to clean out the gutters, trim the trees before winter, change the screens back to storm windows and enjoy a beautiful fall day.

Recently, mother had "those eyes" most of the time. Those eyes that mean they are trying very hard to comprehend the situation and make sense of what is going on around them and it isn't working. There is a short circuit somewhere and it just keeps going round and round in what is left of her brain. She had begun sleeping with her purse, which was mostly empty except tissues and some lip balm. When asked, she said it was to prevent a burglar from getting it. My parents had lived in this same neighborhood for 40+ years without ever having an incident of burglary. Her paranoia was increasing rapidly. She was not safe to be left alone, so father had begun taking her to the grocery store with him. He described her as a "little lost dog" following behind him. He frequently lost her in the store, but it was the local neighborhood grocery and they were well known there. When I had arrived this visit, mother had stated "I won't go to the store again with him" motioning to my father. "Why?". "He hit me in the head the last time we went." When questioned, my father stated that he couldn't get to the lower shelves because of his leg weakness and he was pointing to what they needed and couldn't get mother to pick up the correct box. He had tapped her on the head when her hand got to the proper item. It was becoming obvious that my father was wearing down and his physical health was becoming worse under the strain of care giving. He was now using a walker whenever he walked, including inside the house. I always thought they made a whole human being together. Mother had little brain left, but physically she could do most everything father couldn't. Father had a very sharp brain left, but his body was giving out and his legs in particular, were getting very weak. But now, back to the bag story.

As I said, we had gathered for a great fall day to do jobs around the parent's suburban house. There were grandkids on the roof cleaning out the gutters and others in the trees trimming branches that could cause difficulty in the winter. Others were changing out the screens for storm windows and finally, we got to the part mother really loved, the yard work. We were all dressed in shorts and t-shirts for the job, but mother came out in pants, white snow boots , a jacket, work gloves and a large brimmed gardening hat. When someone asked her if she was too hot, she replied that she was just fine. And so she stayed and worked in her outfit. She couldn't follow the conversations and focus on what she was doing, but she felt the excitement in the air and when we all laughed she laughed also. My father sat on the patio and cried. Then we heard a voice from the roof calling out, "grandma's caught in the bag and can't get out". We all looked over to the patio area and there was one of the tall, heavy duty paper bags that were required for all yard waste. But this bag was upside down and had white snow boots sticking out the bottom. Mother was indeed stuck in a bag. With everyone running to the area, we rescued her from the upside down bag and then deduced what had happened. Actually one of the grandchildren had videoed the entire affair. Mother had been opening one of the very large paper bags that the city gave out for yard waste, and she had decided to open the bag and then put her arms and head into it to "fluff it open". That was when the bag engulfed her completely. She was confused, but laughed because all of us were also laughing. Except my father, who was quietly crying. We took lots of pictures that day of all the family together with my parents. One of my favorite pictures taken that day, is of my mother with those eyes, and her long, scraggly hair tied back with two barrettes. It was that picture that was beside my father when he died. It was Mother, smiling with THOSE EYES.

But………let me start at the very beginning and tell you my mother's story.

Chapter TWO

THE BEGINNING

We were cleaning the windows I had just put up. It was my semi-annual trip back to the Midwest to change out the storm windows to screens in the spring and in the fall, the reverse. Mother was a fanatic about clean windows. It was not an easy job, and I was really tired. She kept insisting that there was a spot on the window, and I cleaned from the outside and then the inside I just wanted to get the cleaning over and leave to visit a friend. All of a sudden mother laughed and took off her glasses. "The spot is on my glasses!! Isn't that too funny." Off she went to clean her glasses and I was left speechless. This was not my mother. This woman never laughed about window cleaning. It was as if an alien had invaded her body. You know, you hear from parents of teenagers that one night their well-behaved, even-tempered child went to bed and their body was invaded by an alien, to be there all through the teenage years. Well, something had invaded my mother and the alien was named dementia. It was an insidious onset; we knew that she was a bit forgetful. We were forever looking for her glasses, and the chain that was supposed to go on the glasses and keep them around her neck so she wouldn't lose them. She couldn't cook the way she used to, and her hair was becoming long, but this was different. Little did I realize that the woman I had not gotten along with all those years was gone. She would never be back. This was just the beginning of a new life for us all.

The beginning.

She was ahead of her time. She used only baking soda and white vinegar and toothpaste to clean things. And lots of physical rubbing and scrubbing. She reused her shopping bags 20 years before it became fashionable and then legislated. She would have been proud.

When she read about coffee being bad for a person, she drank hot water. Just hot water, in the morning with breakfast. She said her father had done it that way.

She always had a slice of lime or lemon in her water. She had seen that in Europe and thought it was good. They had visited Europe when they retired and retraced father's march from D day.

Walking after a meal made the food digest better and then you could have dessert. Used up the calories walking, you know. Mother was an incredible cook and baker. A pie was just an hour away. Entertaining people for a meal was a production and she was very good at it. The table would be set days in advance so we could appreciate the season and the table setting complete with china, usually hand embroidered tablecloth and cloth napkins, and crystal to drink from. Or at least some old glasses from the family once or twice removed, and the table was always truly beautiful.

There was no "down" time. If you were sitting, you would be reading or sewing.OR something.......you could be organizing something. She never took any medication except for the thyroid pill she had taken since I was a small child. She was a wonderful cook and ate only healthy, natural foods. On occasion, she had a glass or two of wine, but certainly she didn't drink daily.

If you had an upset stomach for whatever reason, mother would reach in her purse and give you a piece of crystal ginger. She kept a big piece in her purse always for those emergencies. No purple pill for this lady. We all learned very quickly not to mention upset stomachs in her presence unless we wanted a piece of that nasty tasting stuff.

Let's talk about keeping an active mind. No holiday or family get together was complete until we played games. She loved word games and played them with her dictionary on hand. She was up for learning any new card games and loved spades. At her best, she played bridge at least once a week with the ladies and continued long after her brain could manage it. She didn't go to bed at night until she had read the daily newspaper cover to cover and commented on several of the articles, going so far as to clip out things she wanted us to read and mail them to us. She was also a puzzle freak. When she came for a visit, the kids could count on a 300-piece puzzle to be spread out on the table for the entire visit.

Mother learned to ski when she was in her 50's. She went with some of the neighbors and came back very confident, even though her lips were badly sunburned. She made sure the grandchildren and my sister, and I also learned to downhill ski. Each August, she would begin her "skiing exercises" and spend 30 minutes stretching and working so that she could go skiing in February. Her ashes are spread on her favorite ski mountain per her request. Every time we would ask where she wanted her ashes spread, it was the same answer. There were 13 of us who paid honor to her that sunny day on her favorite ski run.

She was the last person you would think to develop dementia.

Chapter THREE

FACTS AND TREATMENT

I have decided to present some information from several sources regarding the science of dementia. I have utilized information from the National Alzheimer's Association, the National Health Service of the United Kingdom, and the Fisher Center for Alzheimer's Research. There is a plethora of information on the Internet, and you can certainly continue researching the subject. For this book, I have kept the information as simple and accurate as I could.

The National Institute of Neurological Disorders and Stroke defines dementia as:"…[A] word for a group of symptoms caused by disorders that affect the brain. It is not a specific disease. People with dementia may not be able to think well enough to do normal activities, such as getting dressed or eating. They may lose their ability to solve problems or control their emotions. Their personalities may change. They may become agitated or see things that are not there."

Dementia is a general term for a decline in mental ability severe enough to interfere with daily life. Memory loss is an example. Dementia is not a specific disease, rather it is an overall term that describes a wide range of symptoms associated with a decline in memory or other thinking skills severe enough to reduce a person's ability to perform everyday activities. Symptoms of dementia can vary greatly, but at least two of the following core mental functions must be significantly impaired to be considered dementia: memory, communication and language, ability to focus and pay attention, reasoning and judgment, and visual perception. People with dementia may have problems with short term memory, like what happened just a few minutes ago. They may have difficulty keeping track of a purse or wallet, paying bills, planning, and preparing meals, remembering appointments, or traveling out of the neighborhood. Dementia symptoms are progressive meaning that they start out slowly and gradually get worse.

Dementia is caused by damage in the brain. The most common causes of dementia are called neurodegenerative diseases. In these types of diseases, the brain cells degenerate and die more quickly than is part of the normal ageing process. This leads to a decline in a person's mental and sometimes, physical abilities. The gradual changes and damage to the brain cells are caused by a build-up of abnormal proteins in the brain.

Alzheimer's disease is the most common form of dementia, with 60%-80% of patients diagnosed with this particular form of dementia. However, there are several other forms of dementia. The other forms defined below are dementia with Lewy bodies, vascular dementia, and frontotemporal dementia.

As the most common form of dementia, Alzheimers disease is characterized by the loss of brain cells that leads to the brain shrinking. The medical name for this is atrophy. The area of the brain known as the cerebral cortex, or the gray matter covering of the brain, is particularly susceptible to this atrophy, or shrinking. Gray matter is responsible for processing thoughts and many of the complex functions of our brains, such as storing and retrieving memories, calculating, spelling, planning, and organizing.

Here are some statistics regarding Alzheimer's disease: It is the 6th leading cause of death in the United States, with more than 5 million Americans living with the disease. 1 of 3 seniors dies with Alzheimer's or another form of dementia. In 2012, 15.4 million caregivers provided more than 17.5 billion hours of unpaid care valued at $216 billion and 15% of the caregivers for dementia patients are long distance caregivers. In 2013, Alzheimer's will cost the nation $203 billion.

Vascular dementia is caused when the brain's blood supply is interrupted. Like all the major organs, the brain needs a constant supply of oxygen and nutrients from the blood to work well. If the supply of blood is restricted or stopped, the brain cells will begin to die and brain damage will result. Small vessel disease is a subset of vascular dementia caused by the blood vessels of the brain getting clogged with "plaques" or fatty deposits. The blood supply in this case gradually deprives the brain of blood causing brain cells to die.

Dementia with Lewy bodies has similar symptoms as Parkinson's disease. Lewy bodies are small, circular lumps of protein that develop inside the brain cells. No one knows the exact cause or exactly how they damage the brain and cause dementia. People with Lewy body dementia may have difficulty keeping balance and walking and may have shaking of hands and legs. They often have difficulty swallowing and hallucinations, both auditory and visual can occur.

Frontotemporal dementia is caused by damage and shrinking in two areas of the brain. Those two areas are the temporal lobe and the frontal lobe. This is the most common type of dementia seen in people younger than 65 years of age. There may also be muscle wasting with this type of dementia.

No matter the particular type of dementia, the progression of the disease doesn't change and neither does the outcome. DEMENTIA IS A 100% FATAL DISEASE. An analogy from a comedian I heard recently captures this idea perfectly. If you got hit by a car and killed, would it really matter what make or model the car was? Once the diagnosis has been made, the prognosis is the same. Dementia, as a disease process, follows a death curve just like other terminal diseases.

The FDA has approved a number of medications which are safe to treat Alzheimer's disease and can certainly be researched if recommended for your family.

The important thing to know is that *ON AVERAGE, THE FIVE APPROVED ALZHEIMER'S DRUGS ARE EFFECTIVE FOR ABOUT SIX TO 12 MONTHS FOR ABOUT HALF OF THE PATIENTS WHO TAKE THEM.*

Chapter FOUR

HOW DID MOTHERS DOCTORS VISIT GO?

"How did mothers doctors visit go?" I asked the question one day when I called my father. " The doctor was very happy with her tests. She passed!!" Father was very excited about the news. Just how do you pass or fail a dementia test I wondered to myself. "Give me the doctors name father, and I will ask about her results." "No need, she passed, and we are all happy." I could hear the relief in his voice. See, he was thinking, there is nothing wrong with her. As a nurse of 40 years, I knew that there was more to the story.

Mother's behavior had deteriorated since my last visit some 6 months earlier. In that time, there had been some dramatic changes in her behavior and ability to care for herself and my father's ability to care for her. There was the overnight visit with my sister and her family in December when mother didn't pack a coat, and no one noticed until they arrived at their destination. Father had said she had packed and unpacked her suitcase for days and he got "tired" of watching her. He had no idea she had no coat. Add to that the fact that she had brought an outfit that didn't match and had bought the wrong number of tops to pants and no pajamas. This was very uncharacteristic for a lady who was always well organized and had packed for trips through Europe. She was always dressed impeccably, and everything matched. Worse than this was the fact that she wouldn't get her hair cut anymore. Mother had graduated from cosmetology school in her early adult years and still kept her black case with all the permanent rollers, scissors etc. As girls, we had lined up on "permanent day" and included my aunt in all of us getting perms and haircuts. For mother not to allow her hair to be cut was so out of character. Arguing with her only made it worse, as she had decided that she would grow her hair long for donation to an organization to make wigs for cancer victims. But mother's hair was baby fine and falling out at this point in time. Her diet was very poor, and her skin and hair were paying a price. My sister even got mother bandanas and scarves and barrettes for her hair, but nothing made her look anything but unkempt.

Then, there was the time that mother had wanted to go clothes shopping and by this time, father was using a walker to remain mobile. At the department store, he had found a chair to sit in and had promptly lost mother in the sea of racks of clothes. At this time, she stood about 4 foot 8 inches tall and weighed 90 lbs. Thankfully, a lady from the church had recognized mother and had taken her back to where father was seated. The caregiver role and its difficulty was about to rear its ugly head. She had become so different in her behaviors that the entire family could not ignore it anymore. So off to the doctor she went.

I made a call to the doctor and discussed the results of her "tests".

There are basically 2 tests that are easily administered in a doctor's office for patients presenting with symptoms of dementia. The easiest and one that doesn't cause the patient any paranoia is to draw the face of a clock. Examples of such a test are listed below. When I asked mother how she drew the clock face she said, quite triumphantly, "I just put in the 12 and the 6. He's a doctor and is smart enough to know where the other numbers go!" The scoring of this test is done by dividing the clock face into quarters and counting how many of the correct numbers fall into the correct quadrant. Obviously, mother had passed putting just the 12 and the 6 in place. However, it wasn't the passing of the test in the way that she and father understood.

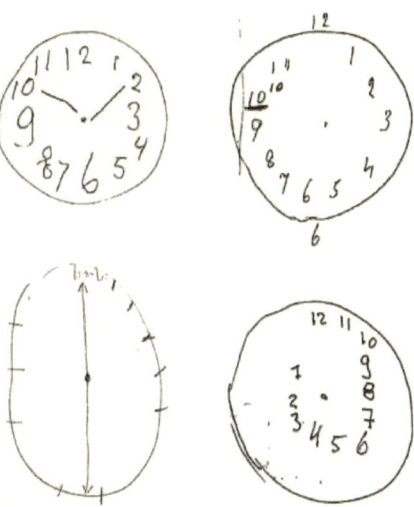

The second test is known as the MMSE or mini mental state examination. It is a simple test composed of several questions in an attempt to discover not only if the patient is affected by dementia, but whether or not any medications would help. It measures a person's memory, attention, and language. 27-30 points is considered normal. Mother had "passed" although her score was in the low 20's or high teens. She was still able to hide symptoms of her disease, mostly from herself and the family. She did not fool the doctor. A sample of the questions from an MMSE test are as follows:

Orientation: what is the date? What holiday is coming up?

Registration: listen carefully. I am going to say three words. You say them back to me after I stop.

Naming: what is this? Pointing to an article, like a pen or pencil.

Reading: here, read this paper and do what it says. A simple task like close your eyes, or smile.

The diagnosis at this point for mother was small vessel dementia. As I said previously in this book, it doesn't really matter what the name of the dementia is, it will follow the same progression and ultimately result in death. Now that we had a diagnosis from a doctor, my father began to acknowledge how she was failing, and we realized that changes were coming faster than anticipated. We were about to begin the later part of the middle phase of dementia. Mother was becoming dangerous to herself. She had the potential to become lost, paranoia was setting in and she could not be safely left at home. My father's life had been limited slightly until now. Soon, he would be a prisoner in his own house with a woman who disliked him and was afraid of him. Worse even, she would begin to forget his name and who he was.

Chapter FIVE

TRAJECTORY

Caught in the middle.

The trajectory of the disease of dementia is a prolonged one and one that has a lot of unknowns. For the purpose of this book, I decided to break down the disease of dementia into 3 phases, early, middle, and late. On the trajectory, the middle phase is the most unpredictable and most difficult for patients and families and may take 2-10 years, so it is the phase we live with the longest. You know that there will be a change coming; you don't know WHEN or HOW, but for a fact, you know WHY and the answer to the why is the disease of dementia. One day, she can dress herself, and pack for a trip and the next day, she can't. She comes out with 3 necklaces on and a top and pants that don't match. And your first thought is to correct what she has done. To make it "normal" and the way it used to be. So, you do that, and she looks at you with THOSE EYES. And you have a choice. THOSE EYES tell about a brain behind them, working through all that you have just said about her appearance and trying to put it into a reality that she can remember..........AND YOU SEE THAT SHE CAN'T. So, you begin to compliment her on how beautiful the necklaces are and suggest a sweater to go over the top for warmth, and she laughs and says, "thank you, I think I will." And she can go out in public with you for the outing you have planned. In the early phase, outings are prized treasures that many families miss or don't even take the opportunity to attempt and enjoy.

" Mother let's go out to lunch. Down in old town and we can go to the shops." Mother loved going to the shops and then to one of the historic restaurants. She had her favorite. So, after she got dressed, as described in the above paragraph, off we went. She had her purse still, but I had encouraged my father to remove the credit cards, except for one and the checkbook. While looking in one of the shops, I picked out a glass ring, orange with recycled glass sparkling on the dome, a stunning piece. Mother said, "I'll get you that for your birthday." She had not remembered my birthday in years, and it certainly wasn't this time of year, but a free ring is a free ring. She managed to get the credit card out and sign her name, as if by rote memory of so many purchases in her lifetime. I watched in amazement as the clerk quietly guided mother through the process. Mother was quite proud also; on a level I can only imagine. Later, on the balcony of her favorite old hotel restaurant, up 3 flights of stairs, by the way, I showed her how the ring glowed in the sunlight. "Ugliest ring I have ever seen." She said. And when I replied that she had just bought it for my for my birthday, she scoffed as if I was lying to her. It was early in the trajectory of this disease. We had a good lunch, although she couldn't manage her sandwich, so I cut it into smaller pieces that she could hold in one hand and eat. She was still able to order from the menu and eat half of her meal. It was a good day.

The middle stage of the disease is distinguished by the loss of "sense of humor" at the symptoms. In the early stage, the patient can usually laugh about what has been forgotten and does not yet have the paranoia of what the disease really is and how it is affecting their ability to participate in daily living activities.

In the early stage, mother wasn't concerned, and we all laughed at what was going on. It was sad, but because she wasn't afraid or particularly worried about what it meant to her future, we were less frightened. Of course, we realized her behavior changes, but were also able to cope with the changes, as they weren't particularly difficult at this stage. Mother wasn't dangerous yet. In the early stages, there are times when reality can be explained, and the demented person accepts the explanation. Friends and family spend a great deal of time trying to reorient the person and reminding them that they are "forgetful". Eventually, this exact behavior contributes to the paranoia of the middle stage of dementia.

One of the last events of the early stage of dementia was when mother and my sister came west for my university graduation. Mother had announced that she was coming to the ceremony, and she would fly out on an airplane by herself.

We knew that would not be possible given her stage of confusion, so my sister agreed to make the trip. By this time, my father wasn't mobile enough to be comfortable with air travel and truth be known, he probably was looking forward to a caregiving break. We still had no idea how much "care" she required. Mother packed and unpacked for a week, something she had always been proficient at. My father attempted to help her, as she would need warm clothing, but this only increased her anger toward his "interference". Having arrived, mother continued to go thru her purse, searching for all the things she thought she might need, some of which she had packed and some not. The day of the graduation, we had a row of seats saved and my sister standing guard awaiting others to come. Mother announced she needed to go to the bathroom and my sister had a moment of "ohmygawd". Could she find her way to and from the bathroom in this huge crowd or would we be looking for her all over the venue. When my sister announced her fears, mother strode off to where she thought the bathroom was and we all prayed she would return. She did manage, but only because another member of the family came upon her looking for the row of seats. After this, we knew life was changing and she would not be safe for much longer. Later in the same visit, my sister and I witnessed something that signaled how much mother was cognitively impaired. Mother had always been a great cook and baking pies was one of her specialties. Knowing that mother needed to be busy, I had given her the job of cutting up apples for one of her famous pies. My sister and I began talking about children and husbands and things and when mother returned with the apples, we were stunned into silence. She had cut the apples into cubes. When asked, she replied that she thought they were "cute and artistic". We made no attempt to "fix" the apples but made the pie and used mother's explanation when the others questioned why the apples were in cubes. That was when everyone realized how impaired she had become and now, how unsafe.

This second phase of the disease can be the longest and most difficult stage of dementia. The demented patient can still do some things, usually by rote memory. Then one day, they lose that ability. The family is left looking for what triggered the change, usually without explanation. You know the change is coming, but not when or how. The changes begin to happen and then the paranoia sets in for the patient. After the first phase, where the family has spent lots of time explaining the "confusion" and inability to do what they used to do, the patient now questions why everyone is against them. Of course, they can do exactly what they used to do, without impairment and then they don't understand why it didn't work like it always has for them. The problem is that in this stage, they begin to become unsafe. You never know what they can or can't do or remember; their name, their address, how to cook. There are a number of steps to be taken now, and most of the steps will increase the paranoia felt by the patient. There is the identity bracelet families can obtain from any one of Alzheimer's groups. Of course, the patient has to keep the bracelet on, which became a problem for us. The bracelet has an emergency telephone number to call if the patient appears to be lost. As an emergency room nurse, I had to call that number a few times to reunite lost families. Mother loved to walk and had walked the same subdivision streets for 40 years. Father was worried when she took off walking that she would become lost. He attempted to follow with the car, but of course, was spotted by mother who was very nasty in her accusations of him "spying on her". This is such an important part of this disease process that I will attempt to break it into a few different phases that we went through and that several of my friends with demented parents went through also. The following are vignettes of my mother's life with the disease and our lives taking care of her and watching her progression.

In the middle stage, the patient knows something is not correct and that they aren't exactly right, but they don't have enough brain power to work through what is wrong and attempt to fix it. It is the "unlearning" stage, as referred to in the book Making Rounds with Oscar by David Dosa, MD. It is the theory that dementia patients are just as busy "unlearning" behaviors that they have learned long ago. Think about how much energy a child puts into learning and then realize that the demented patient is doing the same thing, only in reverse. It is very energy and emotion consuming and they are working really hard at it, unknowingly. Have you ever heard of a caregiver describing the demented person as "very energetic, always moving and very busy. This is the stage where family caring for the person begins to become exhausted. Caring for a demented person is not only physically exhausting, but emotionally exhausting as well. How many times can you be asked, "What is this pill for? What will we eat next? When is dinner ready? The caregiver is worn out trying to explain the reality and then later, ignoring the question because it has been answered too many times with no result. This goes on every day, all day long, except when she sleeps.   Unfortunately, caregivers, especially if they are elder spouses, keep all of this to themselves, fearing that if they tell how bad it is, that the children will want to move them to the "home." And we would have wanted to do that if we had known the whole difficult truth.

Chapter SIX

WOULD YOU EVER

"Would you ever want a feeding tube, mother?" That was a question that I began asking mother on various visits back to the Midwest. I would always ask the question when my father or my sister was in the room, or some of the grandkids. I wanted everyone to hear the answer. "Well why would I want one of those? I'll just eat." Well mother, at some point, your brain will quit thinking about eating and you won't be able to eat. That is why you might want a feeding tube. "I'll just die then if I don't eat." "Then you don't want a feeding tube? Ever?" "NO". That was a short and sweet conversation and thankfully she didn't remember that I had asked her that same question before and that we had had that same conversation, ending the same way. It is this "not eating" that I think signaled the next great decline and it came soon after my last conversation about this feeding tube issue. It is in the trajectory of the disease and death process of dementia that patients quit eating. Mother had really slowed down eating and if food was put before her, she would pick at it, but not eat much. It was as if her brain couldn't remember how to feed herself. A child learns to feed himself as a survival technique from long ago times. The demented patient "unlearns" eating and feeding himself, because it is also a survival technique in a way. The survival is in the ability of the body to begin adapting to the dying process. If left alone, the patient will die a death from kidney failure or pneumonia or urinary infection. They may also develop delirium, a common problem in the demented patient. This is a very difficult period in the trajectory of dementia and in the loved one's acceptance of the finality of the disease. All of a sudden there is a flood of ethical and medical decisions to be made. What if she gets a urinary infection? Should we treat the infection with antibiotics? What is her quality of life, and would she want us to continue this quality for her? These were just a few of the questions that would plague us until the end of mother's life.

There are the questions of surgery and rehab ability if she broke her hip. What would be in her best interest? Putting a patient with dementia in the hospital for any reason causes problems for the staff, as well as the patient and family. Patients get more confused with all of the noise and movement of the hospital, not to mention the painful procedures that hospitalization brings. If the patient requires anesthesia, there can be more problems with increasing confusion and changes in the demented patients ability to follow instructions and just feel safe. All of this burden on both the patient and family makes a case for discussions of these decisions before the patient becomes so demented that they cannot give a truthful answer. I began asking mother about the feeding tube when she was still able to carry on conversations that we knew had meaning. She made herself very clear as to what she would and would not want done in case of a medical dilemma. We knew what she considered good quality of life and also her stated wish of many years to have a "natural death". Mother had a great respect for "natural" things.

Chapter SEVEN

WOULD YOU LIKE

"Would you like to go to the museum, mother?" "That would be wonderful!" she replied in an excited voice. "What do you need to do to get ready?" I asked. " I'll just go in and change my clothes." My father and I sat at the table and had a discussion of something related to how difficult mother was becoming and he denied it was difficult. "She takes naps and that gives me time to go to the grocery or run any errands." he replied. "Is she safe when she wakes up?' Stupid question. "Of course, she is, she just gets busy with one of her projects." We continued the discussion knowing full well that my father was unsure of mothers' safety and that he was wearing down. He was never a patient man and less so now that he was older and being put in a care giving position . An hour later, I went in search of mother, who was changing her clothes to go to the museum. I found her in the master bathroom shower stall, cleaning it with a rag and her usual white vinegar and baking soda mix. When I asked what she was doing, she looked at me in astonishment. "What do you think I am doing?" she asked as she took a break in her scrubbing. "I'm cleaning the shower stall." It was a perfectly reasonable explanation and not worth reminding her that she was supposed to be getting ready to go to the museum. This is the middle part of the disease, which is so difficult for families. She was just beginning to become paranoid every time we corrected her or pointed out that she was supposed to be doing something else. To avoid the situation, I just asked the question again. "Would you like to go to the museum mother?" To which she replied favorably so I just got out a clean shirt and pants for her to put on. We went and had a very enjoyable time. She was still able to go on outings, with supervision, and enjoy them. There is no right or wrong way to live with this "almost" person, who can accomplish things sometimes and other times, she can't be safe in her own place.

Everyone copes with the changing disease and each person copes differently. Those involved with a dementia patient have to do whatever they need to do to have no regrets in the future. Some people consider nursing home placement earlier than others and it isn't more "right or wrong" in the process. This is where guilt may play heavily on the family.. When to make which decisions and what is in the best in interest of the patient and the family. Can the patient be cared for at home, is there enough energy in the care giving group to keep the patient safe and happy? There are no answers written in stone and very little assistance in making those difficult decisions.

Chapter EIGHT

YOUR MOTHER IS

"Your mother is naked in the basement and won't come up the stairs!" I was on my way to visit a home hospice patient when I got this call from my father on my cell phone. "What is she doing down there?" I asked. "She's mad at me and won't answer my questions. She thinks I'm spying on her." My father could no longer get up and down the basement stairs and couldn't risk falling down them to see what mother was doing. "Why don't you call one of the neighbors to help!" I suggested. " I can't let them see her like this!" he said in a very distressed voice. My parents had lived in this same neighborhood for 40 years and all of the neighbors were aware of her dementia and that she was failing. The shame that my father felt for her was honorable and made the situation even more difficult for him. "Have her pick up the phone down there and I'll try talking to her." It was obvious since my last visit that mother was becoming more and more confused and paranoid, and father was not going to be able to care for her much longer without help. Then there was the safety factor. She was becoming unsafe for herself, and we were going to need to take steps to make the house more secure. We had discussed moving them both to an assisted living but had decided that she was less confused in the house she had lived in for 40 years and probably more safe. We worried that moving mother at this point would put her over the edge.   Little did we know how close to that edge we were and that nothing was going to prevent mother from going over into the final phase of dementia. "Mother, what are you doing in the basement?" I asked. " I'm doing laundry, of course." she replied. "Then why are you naked in the basement, mother?" It was obvious that there was more to this situation than I had been led to believe. "I'm washing the clothes that I had on." It seemed so innocent and of course, made perfect sense to her at this point. "Mother, go up the steps right now and leave the laundry. You are needed upstairs right away!" I thought that maybe if I made it an urgent command, she would comply and she did. "Lock the basement door and keep the key in your pocket, father and we will install some hooks and eyes at the top of the door that she can't reach." I placed a call to my sister, who lived close to the parents and told her the story and we decided what was needed to keep mother safe.

We were close to mother going over the edge into the final phase and it took place less than a few days after the above incident. She had not been able to go down the basement steps, but now, she locked herself inside the walk-in closet they had in their bedroom and screamed and called out for help. She said that a strange man had locked her in. My father pleaded with her to unlock the door, but he was the cause of the problem to her. Again, my father was using a walker to avoid falling anymore in the house, and as he unlocked the closet door she ran past him, out the front door and down to the neighbors' house, where she sought refuge and demanded that the police be called. The neighbor called father and he called my sister and eventually, mother was persuaded to return home in the company of my sister, whom she recognized. My father had become a stranger to her, and he cried for a long time over that. We then installed the hooks and eyes on all the doors leading outside, as well as the basement. THEY WERE NOW PRISONERS IN THEIR OWN HOME.

We were obviously at another crossroads. How much longer could mother be kept at home and with what help. Father was having increased difficulty caring for her and she was still quite paranoid and uncooperative with him. We discussed placing mother in a nursing home, but father was adamant that we wait as long as possible for that. We did the numbers and realized that 24/7 help in the home would be about the same price as nursing home care and mothers would be less confused or so we thought. Father would be comfortable in his own home and more safe. He would still have her close by and be able to monitor her failing and would also be safe himself. He was falling more in the home and denying it, but having someone else in the home would make my sister and I much more comfortable. We made a few phone calls to people who had used paid caregivers and contacted the one group that kept being recommended... Yes, they had an opening and some caregivers who would be available. They came to the house to be interviewed and we signed the papers. Now, mother had yet another intruder in her home, who would not leave mother unattended. The situation was rapidly going downhill, but we didn't have any idea it would change drastically within a week.

Chapter NINE

MOTHER JUST

"Mother just hit the caregiver. They have called an ambulance and they are taking her to the emergency room. I'm going up to the hospital now." My sister's voice was full of panic, and she was weary of the time and attention mother's symptoms were taking on father and herself. She had just spent 3 days with them while we made arrangements for a 24-hour, full-time caregiver to be in the house. Mother had seen this woman as an intruder, but she liked the first lady that came to the house. Caregiver #1 cooked and let mother help and included her in some simple tasks. Then they changed caregivers after 48 hours and mother didn't bond with caregiver #2. "I'll call the emergency room and explain things to them." I placed a call to the local emergency room and explained that they were bringing mother in and that I feared she had gotten to the delirium stage of dementia.

I asked that they not do too much in the way of medical technology and that mother had a "Do Not Resuscitate" order from her doctor. I asked that they make sure that there wasn't a urine infection or pneumonia, both of which wreak havoc on a demented persons orientation. If treated, sometimes the patient gets a bit more clear for a short time. Mother had neither and had, in fact, gone over the edge of the disease into delirium and she would have to be placed into a nursing home. Thus began the final phase of mother's dementia. This phase would see her placed in a locked dementia unit in a nursing home and the final 6 months of her life.

It is a dilemma for families at this stage with the question of what has caused this sudden change and what do we do about it? A large number of patients with dementia reach a stage in the disease called "delirium". There are many causes for delirium including electrolyte imbalances caused by decrease in eating and drinking of the patient. There might be an infection, usually urinary tract infections or pneumonias. There is also the fact that deep down inside them, the patient "knows" that something is happening and that there is going to be an event. The event that is anticipated is death, but the demented patient cannot always voice this. They do, however, sometimes refer to "taking a trip", "packing for a journey," or "getting in line for a ticket" These are all references to dying that family members might miss.

Sometimes, adding some sodium in an intravenous solution can help if it is an electrolyte problem, but then there is the confusion of the patient and the chance of falling in the hospital or contracting some other infection while being treated in the hospital. Hospitalization of the demented patient presents problems of its own. Patients have increased confusion, require babysitters or family members at the bedside 24/7 and sometimes the patients fall and break hips in their confusion in the hospital. Then, the family has even more difficult decisions to make. Whether to fix the broken hip, risk anesthesia, which makes dementia worse and then attempt to rehabilitate a patient who cannot follow commands or have the ability to even follow a rehabilitation regime. Families feel guilty and are caught in the difficulty of causing the patient more pain and confusion and what is the actual outcome. Then there is the pressure of others saying, "why wouldn't you fix your mothers broken hip? Will you just let her lay there in pain?" Many of these patients end up in hospice care with an unrepaired hip fracture, on pain medications with the hope of a quiet death.

There is the question of infection, usually a urinary infection or pneumonia, which can cause a sudden change in behavior in those with dementia. Sepsis is an infection from one source that enters the bloodstream of the patient spreading the infection to other organs of the body. Both pneumonia and urinary tract infections can be treated with antibiotics and the patient may get more alert for a short period of time. However, continued infections cause the family to question treatment for the infection. Death by sepsis is not uncommon in patients with dementia and is usually a quiet death.

However, delirium changes the game entirely. The patient cannot usually be cared for at home safely without

24/7 caregivers. Family quickly realizes that the patient doesn't resemble the person she was and therefore, cannot be reasoned with. Delirium causes the patient to confuse day and night and many patients are awake and moving all night, exhausting caregivers in the home. These patients may become physically threatening to family, not recognizing them. Dementia patients are very powerful physically in spite of their small and frail stature and can do harm to family or themselves in an effort to "escape" from a situation that they see as "harmful" to them. These patients in delirium are trying desperately to "fight" for their lives and their very existence. They see anyone who doesn't understand as the enemy. There are medications used for delirium, which may or may not help make the patient more manageable and safer. However, these medications may make the patient "doped up" and very sleepy and many families think that this is a worse choice than the delirium. These patients are very physically active with energy unbounded in an effort to "get to the train" on time. It is a heartbreaking end for loved ones who have cared for the patient until this time.

We were now entering the final stage of dementia. Mother could not be cared for at home by father and the 24/7 caregivers that we had tried for a week. She had to be placed into a nursing home for safety. "What do I do now?" My sister had called when they were leaving the emergency room. She had agreed to stay yet again with the parents until the issue was resolved. My father could no longer handle mother. "Get the phone book and begin calling all of the nursing homes, sister. Ask if they have a locked unit for dementia patients and if they have an open bed." We prayed for a solution to come our way. This is one of the situations that can be planned for in advance, but we were caught very unaware of the difficulty and immediacy of the situation. On call number 3, my sister talked to the actual administrator of a local nursing home, who comforted her and made her feel like this facility could handle mother. We were aware of the nursing home because another elderly relative had spent some time there. They were willing to take mother into their locked unit and they had an opening. The original caregiver came back to stay the night and give my sister a break. The following day, mother, accompanied by my father and caregiver, entered the door of the nursing home and the door locked behind them. Mercifully, mother did not ask to go with them when they left. She was already oblivious to the situation and her confusion was markedly increased due to the delirium and the medication used to control the delirium.

Within a day of her admission, I received a call stating that they had found mother on the floor looking for something. I thought no, she is washing the floor. My mother was a cleaner and was fastidious about clean floors. They requested to move her to the "other" locked unit, for those patients who needed one on one observation. Of course, I gave permission for her move, and then thought about what to do in case of a fractured hip. I needed for my sister and father to be on the same page, and they were. We would not subject mother to hospitalization and surgery. The same day mother was admitted to the nursing home, I contacted the local hospice and she entered into hospice care for her last 6 months of life. That same day, we put mother into what is known as a "low bed" basically a mattress on the floor, so as to decrease her incidence of falling out of bed and fracturing her hip. There was also a "fall mat" next to the bed which consisted of a thick rubber mat, similar to those used in tumbling. In the event that mother did manage to slip out of the bed, she would fall only a few inches into the mat. In the next few days, mother spent more time on the mat then she did the bed. She always seemed to be looking for something she had lost. It is a common trait of the last phase of dementia, the delirium that the patient lives in until the end.

Chapter TEN

WHAT HAPPENS

"What happens to all of your mother's clothes? What about her face cream and hair curlers?" Mother had been placed in the locked dementia unit of a local nursing home the week before and this was my first call from my father. It was obvious that he was overwhelmed. The woman he had lived with for some 60 years was not in his house anymore, but all of her "stuff" was. The "stuff" that made her normal for all those years. The things that she relied on daily. "What will we do with her jewelry?" he asked. Of course, all of her clothes were still in the closet and dresser drawers. Placing mother had happened so quickly, none of us had thought about the "after placement" chores that have to be performed. " I'll come back in a few days father, and we will get everything taken care of." He seemed ok with the prospect of living with her "stuff" until I got there. My sister and I coordinated a date, and I made the reservations to fly back another time. Dispersing the "stuff" of a person who still lives but is not in need of any of her things was a stark realization for me. Mother was now being cared for in a locked unit in a nursing home, where they dressed her in the warm clothes we had brought. Of course, we had taken her underclothing when we packed her things for the nursing home, not exactly sure what we were thinking. She was incontinent of urine and stool now since the delirium had set in. She needed only diapers now and staff to wash her and clean her when she was wet or dirty.

Mother had prided herself on her beautiful clothing when she was still alert and oriented. Several times, I had asked what should be done with all those beautiful dresses and shirts when she no longer wore them. She had not been dressed up and taken out in several years. There was a charity in town that gave clothes to women new to the work force or those trying to get jobs and mother had voiced support for that charity and its mission. We dutifully loaded up her clothes and took them to the little house that held the charity and the clothes. We felt that we were carrying out mothers wishes and felt sad, but good about doing that. Father avoided the bedroom when we were going through all the clothes and cleaning out the dresser drawers. It was too much to see what was left of the "love of his life" going out of the house in boxes and in the back of our cars. We opened the jewelry boxes and began looking over the pieces and dividing them up between the daughters and granddaughters. Father gave a history of some of the antique pieces, as mother was the "catch all person" for all of the old jewelry and family pieces. Going through all of her purses caused lots of tears and laughter around the table, as we shared stories of the purses and hats that mother had accumulated. Gradually, we made it into a bit of a celebration of remembering her as she was then, not as she had become now.

Chapter ELEVEN

HOSPICE

Hospice is one of the three forms of medical care in the United States, the others being acute and palliative care. Hospice care has been in the states for about 50 years and focuses its energy on the comfort and dignity of the patient and the inclusion of the family as part of the patient and the patient's care. Hospice is defined by the Medicare reimbursement definition that is "if the disease is allowed to take a natural course, the patient will be dead in 6 months". However, in dementia, the time limit is not the only qualification because the dementia death curve is so very diverse and different for each patient. There are other criteria for a dementia diagnosis in hospice including the loss of function, loss of weight, and inability to care for oneself, multiple infections requiring treatment, and delirium. Hospice entered mother's world the day after she was placed in the nursing home. Since I was a hospice nurse already, I knew that she would qualify for hospice care based on the events of the past week, with the emergency room visit and diagnosis of delirium. Mother would still answer to her name and some days she was able to participate in some conversation. That quickly disappeared and she became confined to the wheelchair, sitting in the dayroom and sometimes participating in some of the therapy groups. We were finally able to get her hair cut, but my sister had to stay with mother in the beauty shop at the nursing home. This from a woman who had spent her early adult years as a beautician and had always had perfectly coiffed hair.

Then, another difficulty began for us. No one would visit mother. Everyone said they didn't want to remember her as the babbling woman in the wheelchair. My father couldn't bring himself to visit much and when he did, had to sit on the opposite side of the room as mother still didn't like him even though she didn't know who he was. My sister had two jobs and lived an hour away, so her trips were limited. She was hurt that no one would visit. This is a difficult time for family and friends: the dilemma of whether to visit or not. Some people say that they don't want to remember her like that, but this isn't the lasting memory of the person you once knew. As we reflect on that now, we remember all the times she was at the sports games with the grandchildren and all of the entertaining she did. The memory of the babbling woman in the wheelchair is faded. Each time we visited, the entire unit of perhaps 10 patients would crowd around the table, starved to have discussions with people that they thought were visiting them. For those who do not visit, I would say this. They have to continue on without regret having not visited in the last phase of the disease. Visitors to my parent's house had dropped off to nothing at this point. My parents were isolated by her disease and prisoner in their own home. To have no one visit, especially now when she was in the nursing home, was almost an insult to her memory and that insult was felt by the family. Mother deserved better than that and would have visited any of her friends so confined. . Mother did have one of her oldest friends visit and that did make things a bit easier for the local family. That someone had recognized the person in the nursing home with dignity and friendship. Someone who had known her in her best days, as well as these, her worst.

I was the long-distance daughter, calling usually during the night shift, when I was working. I developed a rapport with the night nurse on the unit. Every night I worked I called to inquire if medications were needed and how mother was reacting. God bless the connection of night nurses all over the world.

Then there was the excellent hospice nurse who updated me once a week on mother's regression. I remember her telling me that mother was textbook for dementia, and she was certainly declining at a rapid pace. There were times when my father would go visit for lunch and he would be so happy that mother had eaten a few bites. I could never get him to understand the death curve of the disease and that not eating was going to happen.

At this point, we did not realize how vulnerable mother was. Just because she was in a secure place with 24/7 care, we didn't realize that she couldn't make her needs known. She was becoming less and less verbal, and her voice was just a whisper. Families at this point need to remember to keep "eyes" on the patient to see if she is eating, able to say when she needs something, like going to the bathroom, or being cold or hot. My sister came to the unit one day to find mother blue and cold and shivering in her wheelchair. It was apparent that she could not communicate that she was cold and needed warmer clothes on. After that, my sister and I posted signs above her bed asking that they dress her warmly.

Sometimes we would visit to see someone else on the unit wearing one of mother's outfits. This happens commonly in locked dementia units where the patients wander in and out of the rooms. Some families are bothered by this behavior, but we decided not to make that an important point for us. As long as mother was always dressed warmly, we were grateful. She weighed maybe 80 pounds at this time. She had begun to keep her eyes closed all the time. It was obvious that the outside world didn't make much sense to her anymore, so tuning it out worked best for her.

There are 2 other situations that families need to pay attention to and consider. One is the need to look at the chair the patient is in. Does it support them and the need they have for   movement and support. When mother entered the nursing home, she could pedal the wheelchair around with her feet. She could no longer stand and be safe to walk.   As mother's disease progressed, she required more support to sit upright in the chair, so we moved to a "geri chair" a large stuffed chair that had a table to fasten in front of her to hold her food and anything else to occupy her such as folding washcloths. Much sooner than we thought, she required pillows to prop her upright in the padded chair and then, she could no longer sit in an upright position, so the chair reclined just enough to keep her in an upright position.

When mother entered the nursing home, she was still able to feed herself with encouragement. Soon after she began to just look at the food and required feeding assistance. Then as the disease continued, mother began to just keep the food in her mouth, called "pocketing of food" and she forgot how to swallow. Father was always happy when he was visiting, and mother was able to swallow a few bites of food given her by the nursing staff. I couldn't get him to understand that the food she was taking in at that point would not sustain her life, but food is so basic to "caring" in our culture. This is when the question of a feeding tube may present itself to the family and the decision was made that mother never wanted a feeding tube and we would not even consider such a procedure.

Another part of hospice care is the chaplain and social worker assigned to each patient and also a nurse assistant to bathe her twice a week. All of these people added a level of care and extra eyes on both mother and my father. The chaplain especially assisted my father through the grief process and validated my father's loyalty to his stricken wife. Those conversations helped my father immensely. The chaplain also sang hymns to my mother who would tap her foot to the beat and when he said some common prayers with her she was able to mouth a few words with him. The social worker assisted my father in the Medicaid requirement for payment in nursing homes. A further explanation of Medicaid can be found in the caregiver section later in this book.

One day I got a call from the hospice nurse who said that mother had probably had another stroke, or series of strokes and was now unable to sit up in the wheelchair and she was not able to swallow to eat, even being fed. She kept the food in her mouth. This is called "pocketing food" and is very common in the last stages of dementia. Mother had entered her dying phase. When I saw her a few days later, the decision was made that mother no longer needed to be gotten up and dressed, which is a requirement of nursing homes for their residents.

It took a day or two to discuss medications with my father and sister. Mother had delirium and now could no longer take the pill for that. Hospice care concentrates its efforts on making the patient comfortable. I talked to my father and sister about comfort medications and the fact that mother was dying, and she deserved to be comfortable and not afraid. She was begun on liquid Morphine and Ativan for the pain and the anxiety she might be having. This was a very difficult decision for my family, and I think that most family members find this decision uncomfortable. Are we hastening her death by giving her morphine, or are we making her comfortable in her final days? This is yet another ethical dilemma for families to talk over. We could not change mothers' course at this point, it was a waiting game for her death and not a comfortable place to be. She died 13 days later, a very long and arduous time for all of us. We knew that she was comfortable and in no distress that we could detect. We took turns at her bedside assuring her it was soon to be over and that she would soon be whole again. It was a peaceful death.

I want to mention something about grief, because grief is different in the death of someone with dementia. The family and loved ones have grieved sometimes for years, as the person they knew has been dead to them for some time. When the actual physical death occurs, there may be some feelings of relief for the patient who will be whole again and who has suffered immensely through the disease. Then the family may feel guilty for feeling that way. We certainly did. As a hospice nurse, I have witnessed a number of dementia deaths and families are very conflicted in their feelings because of this double- edged sword of grief.

There is another fact that is little known and that is that dementia deaths may take a longer time than those of other diseases. I had a social worker at the hospice explain her thoughts on this. She would always pray for an angel to come help the dying demented patient because she thought that they were too confused to "go to the light". They see it but can't understand what they need to do. In death, just as in life, there is confusion. It is an accepted fact in hospice that when we would have a demented patient admitted we would try to brief the family on this type of behavior at the end of life for patients with dementia.

Chapter TWELVE

IN GOOD TIMES

"In good times and bad, in sickness and in health, for richer, for poorer, as long as we both shall live". They took these vows very seriously. They had survived the great depression, the war to end all wars, the great increase of national wealth and the suburbs and now, they were being called upon to survive one last battle. That battle was the caregiving of the demented person they had married 50+ years before. Statistics about the caregivers for those with dementia state that in 2012 15.4 million caregivers provided more than 17.5 billion hours of unpaid care valued at $216 billion. Nearly 15% of caregivers for people with Alzheimer's or another dementia are long distance caregivers. Most of the caregivers are elderly spouses of those patients with dementia who are helped by other family members. For this book, I will focus on that last fact, which was our situation. My father was not a born caregiver but grew into the role because he had promised he wouldn't quit. He was so ashamed for anyone to see mother and what she had become. He protected her until he couldn't do it anymore. He had promised to keep her at home until the end but didn't realize what that end would look like.

What I realize, as I look over the 10 years of his caregiving, is the loss that he suffered as a result of mother's illness. As she became more confused and argumentative, the invitations to dinners with friends decreased and then stopped. Going to their favorite restaurant might result in finding a biscuit or some other part of the meal in her purse. Mother loved going to musical productions, often at the local high school and junior college, but this too was lost when she could no longer be taken out in public. Father has described her as a "lost little dog" walking behind him in the grocery store, so you can imagine what it was like to take her out into the public. I described in one of the previous chapters him losing her in the department store when she insisted on going shopping for some new clothes.

Mother had always sung in the church choir and she and my father were always very involved with church activities. At some point, we really don't quite remember, mother could no longer read the music to sing in the choir and soon after, her voice became weak and scratchy. I remember the day she told me she couldn't sing anymore with that voice, and I tried to explain it as part of her disease. But at this point in time, she wasn't convinced she had a disease. Soon, the socialization of the church and its activities was lost in mother's fog. Father didn't bother to tell her what day it was but would ask if she wanted to listen to a "church service" on the radio. Sadly, it was the service they would have attended in person had they been able. The service was broadcast on a local radio station to accommodate all of the "shut-ins" who were members of the church.

When mother became unable to go out in public, they became prisoners in their own home. My father escaped via his television and satellite dish, which mother hated. As her disease progressed, father watched it more and more and let mother travel the house, knowing that she couldn't escape as the doors were secured now. My father even kept away from the neighbors of 40 years so that they wouldn't know how difficult she had become. He also hid most of this from my sister and myself because if we had known the whole truth, we would have insisted on moving mother earlier than we did.

There are some things that you must consider if you find yourself in our situation. The first is advance planning. What is it that the patient wants and doesn't want done in the name of medicine. Mother rarely went to doctors and didn't take many medications, except for her thyroid pill. She was a whole food, natural remedy person well before her time. It was a daily routine for my father to hear, "what is this pill for?" Every morning, he would explain the vitamins, the herbs she had taken for years and the little thyroid tablet. She had refused to add the "orange one" to her regime, which was the Alzheimers medication that we were going to try. Rather than have my father fight the "orange pill" battle each day, we didn't even try the medication. Percentages of medication victory over the disease are very low and usually only hold off the confusion symptoms for a short time. I asked mother every time I visited if she would want a feeding tube and the answer was always a firm no. However, there are other advance planning points that need to be considered. In the later stages of dementia, chronic infections, usually pneumonia or urinary infections, plague the patient. Infections can be treated with antibiotics and usually this is the case in the early stages. However, it becomes an ethical dilemma for families when the infections are recurrent, and the antibiotics become ineffective. The question of "prolonging life, or prolonging death" and quality of life become evident to families and other caregivers.

The other difficulty of treatment is whether or not to do surgery on a demented person for either a fractured bone, usually a hip from a fall, or the bowel obstructions that causes pain and would normally require surgery for healing. However, the surgery and anesthesia themselves cause difficulty for the patients with dementia, usually making the confusion worse. Then there are safety factors of hospitalizing dementia patients and the fear factor and falling factor. These patients can't make sense of the normal world they live in, how can we expect them to make sense of the acute care hospital environment, with the buzzers and bells and noise levels as well as the "hustle and bustle" of all the staff coming in and out of their room. With increased activity that is senseless, the paranoia may increase, or delirium may set in. Either case requires a sitter in the acute care facility or family to sit with the patient 24/7 for safety. These are not easy choices for families to make.

Sundowners is a common symptom in the later stages of dementia. It is when a patient gets their days and nights mixed up and they tend to be up and "busy" all night and then catnap during the day. Families have a tendency to blame this on medications or moving patients to another facility or from home to a nursing home. This is the stage where caregivers in the home cannot keep the patient at home without 24/7 caregivers because normal people need to sleep. It is very difficult to keep up with an 80-year-old female who is walking all around the house at all hours of the night. Safety becomes impossible and things happen when caregivers don't have enough sleep. People need to understand that this is part of the disease process and that medications only make the patient manageable. These patients are paranoid and can very well hit and harm the caregivers or other patients. Again, this is the trajectory of the disease and even with noble intentions, the family cannot prevent the disease from continuing.

My parents had completed medical power of attorney papers{ MDPOA} as well as living wills early in their lives, well before mother was diagnosed. Both had then obtained DO NOT RESUSCITATE orders from their physicians soon after the mothers' diagnosis. All of these were done at my sister and my insistence, and my parents realized the importance of advance planning. Not only advance planning needs to occur, but there are the financial difficulties that come with the diagnosis of the disease.

Medicare, which is the insurance for those over 65, does not pay for room and board in a nursing home.

Medicare does not pay for the cost of keeping patients in a room with meals and medications being dispensed. This is considered "custodial care" and is not a covered benefit. To get this part paid for, there is long term care insurance, which covers the cost of room and board, and for others, there is the Medicaid program. Those who have long term care insurance must read carefully the percentage of room and board coverage. Many policies are different in what they cover exactly. Those who qualify for "Medicaid only" already will have their custodial care paid for. Medicaid only means that this is the only way of payment for the patient's medical needs. However, only some nursing homes take Medicaid payment and others facilities dedicate only a few beds for those receiving only Medicaid payment so there are usually waiting lists at these facilities. The reason that all nursing facilities don't take "Medicaid only" patients is because that particular federal program pays so very little of the actual cost of custodial care. There is also the hospice benefit of Medicare which pays for medications, equipment, and staff, but those patients must be qualified for hospice care and there are specific criteria patients have to meet for that benefit.

There was another option under Medicaid that fit the situation of my parents. Medicaid is based on the assets held by the patient and in my parents' case, they had a car, a house and several investments, pensions and 401 k programs. My mother had too much money to have her custodial care paid for, so my father, with the assistance of the social worker in hospice, began what is known as the "spend down" of my mothers' half of the assets. The embarrassment of my father having to reveal the entirety of his earthly wealth to a complete stranger was so very difficult for him. However, by the time my mother was confined to the locked dementia unit in the nursing home, my father was at the mercy of the system and was not to be defeated by it.

Chapter THIRTEEN

DEATH TRAJECTORIES

Death curves are commonly used in the practice of medicine. For those of you who consider the discussion of death philosophically or theologically uninteresting to you, take note. Here is the discussion of death in black and white. Graphs and perpendicular lines and everything mathematically needed for your understanding of the term "death". Every terminal disease has a progression graph, from the time of diagnosis until the end of the disease which results in death. There are 4 of them listed in this chapter. One might ask the question why have death trajectories in a book about dementia? The answer is a simple one. DEMENTIA IS A FATAL DISEASE.

The first graph is the sudden death curve where there is an event causing sudden death. A trauma perhaps or a heart attack or massive stroke would be examples of this type of death. The avalanche or the gunshot wound in a botched robbery. It is sudden, unanticipated. You are alive along the top of the curve, then the event occurs, and death follows.

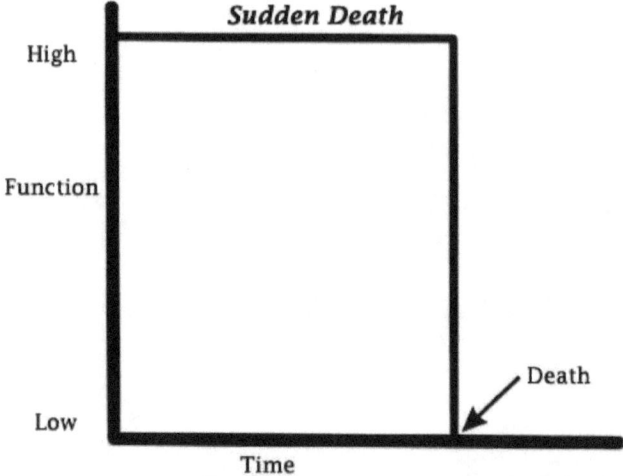

The second death curve is that of terminal illness. An example of that would be cancer, where you are alive, maintaining with treatment and then there comes a time when treatment is no longer effective and there is a fairly sudden downward spiral toward death in a few weeks. It is at this sudden downward spiral that many people enter the world of hospice for their final days/weeks.

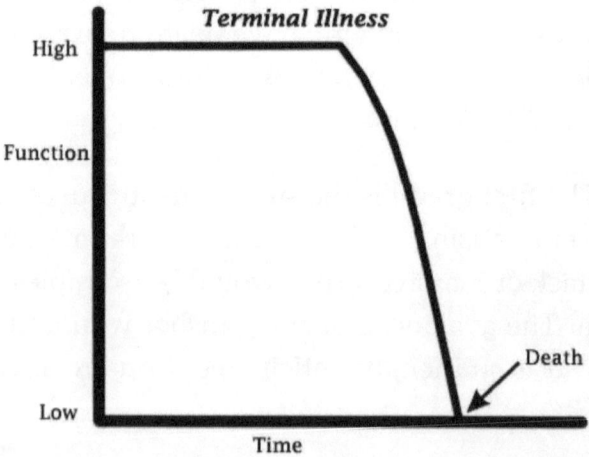

The third death curve is that of a chronic illness, where the patient lives well for a while, has an exacerbation of the disease, and goes downward in the living spiral. Examples of a chronic disease would be COPD or chronic obstructive pulmonary disease. An exacerbation is defined as an intensity of symptoms of a chronic disease, like the shortness of breath that comes with COPD. The patient is able to come recover, usually with hospitalization and treatment of some kind. You will notice that the patient never gets all the way back to the quality of life he had previously, the "high function" on the graph, because after each exacerbation, the patient has less energy and is more ill than before his exacerbation. His disease process is worsening but can still be "treated", though not cured.

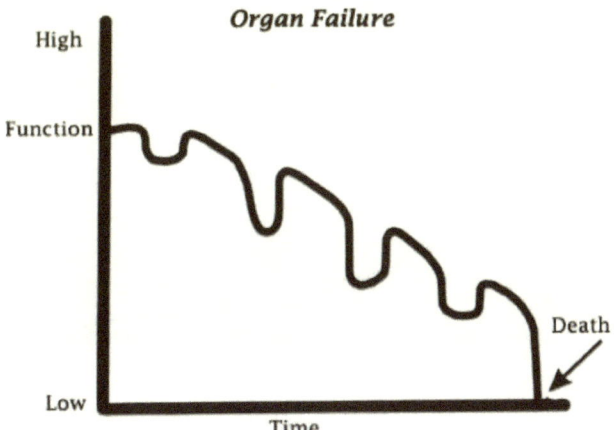

Then there is the death curve of dementia, which is labeled "frailty" in this graph. You will note that it goes in a continuously downward trend, but there are some sudden downward spikes in the curve with the progression of the disease process. Please understand that dementia is a FATAL disease. The trajectory is marked with sudden downward movements and then a plateau or stabilization of symptoms. I have labeled these times on the trajectory as the "inbetween" times of the disease. You know there will be changes and loss of function and memory. You just don't know when these changes will come and how drastic they will be, but you can be assured that changes will occur and that once something has been lost it will usually not come back in a meaningful way.

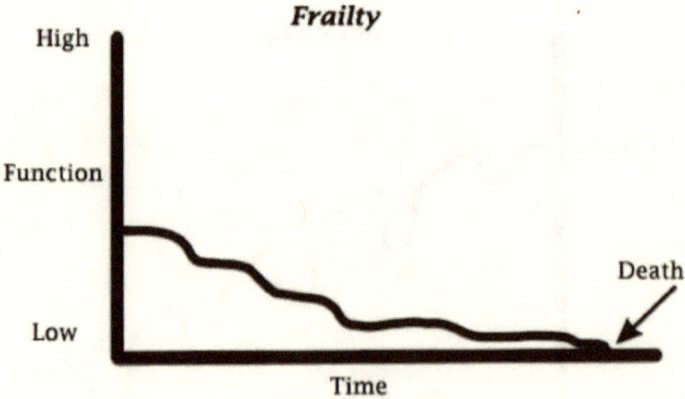

Chapter FOURTEEN

THE ENDING

So why write this book? Why tell mothers story and use it to spread some information about the disease of dementia, the difficulty of the disease for those who live with it and caregivers who watch over those with the disease? Perhaps because I begin to ask some questions that I don't think are different than those asked by other sons and daughters of demented parents. And those questions are:

What are the odds that I will get the disease?

What can I do to extend my "normal life"?

What decisions will have to be made and who will make them?

What paperwork do I need to do so that my family doesn't have to be burdened with making those decisions on top of caring for me?

If I am at increased risk for developing dementia, should I live my life differently now, while I still have my faculties?

I wrote mother's story after my first book, which is the link between the two. My first book, *Discussions, A Guide To Navigating Healthcare Choices* is about those decisions that will need to be made and the paperwork to fill out. It addresses the discussions to have with the family and friends that will eventually hold the burden of your care. Mother lived each day to its fullest not ever considering that her time would be so limited and so severely disabled. That is a lesson that we should all learn because we who are at increased risk of the same fate need to live fully now.

www.ingramcontent.com/pod-product-compliance
Lightning Source LLC
LaVergne TN
LVHW041222080526
838199LV00082B/1874